DIY Flower Arranging for Kids: Bc

By Mercedes Sarmini

DIY Flower Arranging for Kids: Book 1

By Mercedes Sarmini

Flowers By Mercedes ABN 64 132 108 153

PO Box A163, Enfield South, Sydney NSW 2133

Telephone: (02) 9797 8811 Fax: (02) 9787 8447

Email: info@FlowerArrangingForKids.com

Web: www.FlowerArrangingForKids.com

First published in 2009.

National Library of Australia

Cataloguing-in-Publication entry:

Sarmini, Mercedes

DIY flower arranging for kids (electronic resource): Book one

9780980596915 (pdf.)

Flower arrangement--Juvenile literature
745.92

Design and Typesetting by Mercier Typesetters, Granville NSW.

Thank you

Thank you for purchasing this Book. We want to create many more like it so that we can fill this world with beautiful, colourful flowers.

I hope you agree.

So to keep on making more of these Books we need to know how much you like our work.

We would love it if you could give us an honest REVIEW.

That way we can make each Book better than the last one

Also remember that you can download your Free Flower Arranging Videos at http://www.FlowerArrangingForKids.com

"good things come to those who flower"

-Mercedes

About the Author

With 14 years floral experience, Mercedes Sarmini has taken the Floral Arranging Industry by storm. She is the proud owner of a thriving Sydney Floral Boutique as well as the Founder of Flowers by Mercedes, a Worldwide Floral Training Academy.

At the young age of 10, Mercedes' entrepreneurial talents were activated by the beauty she saw in flowers and floral arranging. It was at this tender age that she began creating a small income at the markets, from her love of the colours, shapes and fragrance of cut flowers.

Mercedes Sarmini is a Pioneer in the Floral Arranging for Kids market. As a qualified childcare Assistant and with her knowledge of floristry, Mercedes has been able to combine the two industries together and deliver floral arranging for Kids in the form of workshops and an educational (yet fun) eBook series.

"So what are you waiting for? Isn't it time you got Floral?"- Mercedes Sarmini

Download your Free Flower Arranging for Kids Video Projects today by visiting

http://www.FlowerArrangingForKids.com

CONTENTS

Red and yellow and pink and green,
purple and orange and blue
I can make some flowers, lots of flowers
Let me show you how to!

Statement of the Rainbow

The Children Are Our Future

Each bow of the rainbow represents the 7 gifts that children bring to our lives:

Joy, hope, happiness, laughter, prosperity, togetherness and unconditional love.

Remember, children are our future and like the colours of the rainbow, together, let's add colour to their lives.

Acknowledgements

I would like to thank God and my mother, without them, this book would not have been possible. I would like to thank all the people and children who believed in my floral dream and backyard floral arranging concept.

And last, I would love to thank my daughters, Dania and Sabrina for volunteering their floral time to the making of this book.

Make a start, make a difference and remember, good things come to those who flower!

Mercedes Sarmini

Psst! Floral arranging feeds the soul. It's productive. It's therapy!

In loving memory of Connie Silvio.

Flowers in the Box

Flowers in the Box

Flower Ingredients

• Tulips –Orange and Yellow

• Roses –Apricot

• Moss

• Molucca Balm

Flower Equipment

• Timber Box

• Paint –Orange, Yellow and Red

• Bowls• Sponge Paint Brushes

• Moving Craft Eyes

• Wooden Ladybirds

• 22 gauge Wire

• 2 Floral Foam Bricks

• Butter Knife• Cellophane –Clear

• Secateurs

• Table Protection Sheet

• Container

Method

1. Place timber box on table protector, and with your orange, red and yellow paint standing in bowls, collect the paint with your sponge paintbrush, and start painting the timber box to your liking.
2. Apply moving craft eyes and wooden ladybirds onto dollops of paint, to guarantee hold.
3. Allow drying overnight or you may blow-dry with hairdryer to accelerate the process.
4. Measure the Floral Foam bricks to the timber box, before cutting.
5. Line the timber box with clear cellophane to stop leakage.
6. Apply the cut floral foam bricks into a container of deep cold water and allow to stand for 3 minutes.
7. Place the wet, cut to size floral foam brick into the timber box.
8. Cover the wet Oasis with moss and secure with pinned wire.
9. Trim the orange and yellow tulips, molucca balm and apricot roses with your secateurs and place in groups into the moss covered floral foam brick.
10. Garnish with rose petals or bloomed tulip heads around the timber box.

(Substitute other flowers if flower ingredients are not available)

P.S. Makes a great gift for Mother's Day and Birthdays.

a. place the paint, ladybirds and craft eyes in dishes ready for use

b., c. & d. paint the timber box to your liking

c.

d.

e. soak paint brushes after use

f. apply ladybirds and moving eyes onto dollops of paint

g. allow timber box to dry before use

h. measure dry floral foam brick to timber box before soaking

i, j & k. measure and cut the dry floral foam bricks before soaking

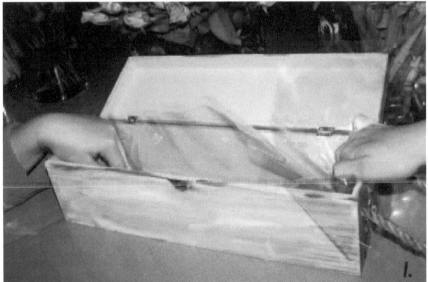

l. line the timber box with clear cellophane

m. place dry floral foam brick into a container of deep, cold water

n, o. ensure the floral foam is completely covered with water and allow to soak for 3 minutes

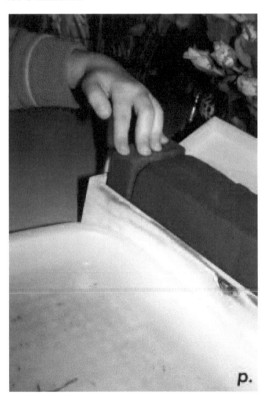

p. cut away any excess and place into timber box

q.

r.

q, r, s & t. cover the wet floral foam with moss and secure in place with pinned wire.

U.

V.

u, v & w. trim orange and yellow tulips, molucca balm and apricot roses with your secateurs and place in groups into the moss covered floral foam brick

x. garnish with rose petals or bloomed tulip heads

Flaming Flower Kebabs

Flaming Flower Kebabs Rated PG

Flower Ingredients

• Mini Gerbera – Hot Pink and Orange

• Mini Capsicum –Red and Green

• Mini Mild Chilli Peppers

Equipment

• Mini Skewers

• Plastic Lime Green Party Plates

• Fork and Knife

• Secateurs (optional)

Method

a. Hold upright one mini skewer and start threading onto the skewer red and green mini capsicums. Leave enough space for some gerberas and chilli peppers.
b. Using your fingers, snap the gerbera heads off the stem or cut them with your secateurs.
c. Now thread the gerbera heads onto the mini skewer.
d. Next, thread the skewer with the mild chilli peppers.
e. Keep repeating the process until the mini skewer is fully loaded.
f. Set up the table with your party plates and cutlery.
g. Place the Flaming Flower Kebabs onto the party plates.
h. Garnish with remaining capsicums and gerbera heads.

CAUTION: Wash your hands thoroughly after completing this activity and keep your hands away from you

(Substitute other flowers if flower ingredients are not available)

P.S. Makes a great gift for Teddy Bear Picnic Party & Australia Day.

a. group all your materials together

b. start threading red and green capsicums onto the mini skewer

c. cut gerbera heads off the stems

d. thread gerbera heads and then mild chilli peppers onto the mini skewer

e, f. repeat the same process until the skewer is full of capsicums, gerbera heads and mild chilli peppers

g. arrange skewer onto party plate with cutlery

h. garnish with remaining capsicums, mild chilli peppers and gerbera heads

Hundreds of Thousands of Flowers

Hundreds of Thousands of Flowers

Flower Ingredients

• Jonquils –Yellow

Flower Equipment

• Toilet Paper Roll	• Coaster
• Craft Glue	• Hundreds & Thousands
• Secateurs	• Tin Tray
• Camera Film Container	• Bowl

Method

1. Pour hundreds & thousands into a bowl.

2. Squeeze craft glue onto a rectangular tray.

3. Roll the toilet roll into the tray of glue until the toilet roll is covered.

4. Next, take your glue covered toilet roll and roll it into the bowl of hundreds & thousands.

5. Once the toilet roll is covered, allow it to dry overnight standing on a coaster or blow dry with a hairdryer on cool setting.

6. Insert camera film container into the hundreds & thousands covered toilet roll and fill half the container with cold water.

7. With your secateurs, cut the jonquils to size and place in the camera film container.

8. Garnish with hundreds & thousands and jonquil flower heads.

(Substitute other flowers if flower ingredients are not available)

P.S. Makes a great gift for Mother's Day & Daffodil Day.

a. place hundreds& thousands in a bowl. Squeeze glue onto a rectangular tray. Roll the toilet roll through the glue so it is covered

b, c. roll the glue covered toilet roll through the bowl of hundreds & thousands

d. allow the toilet roll to dry overnight

e. half fill the film container with water and place the toilet roll over the top

f, g. cut jonquils to size and place into the film container inside the toilet roll

h. garnish with hundreds & thousands and jonquil heads

Incy Wincy Flower

Incy Wincy Flower

Flower Ingredients

• Spider Orchid

Flower Equipment

• Turkish Coffee

• Sultanas• Glass Baby Food Jars x 3

• Table Protection Sheet

• Secateurs (optional)

Method

1. Cover your table with a protection sheet.
2. Place your 3 empty glass baby food jars on the table with the lids off.
3. Pour 1/3 of the packet of sultanas into each jar, keeping a few sultanas for garnishing.
4. Using your fingers, snap off the spider orchid from its stem or you may use secateurs for this exercise.
5. Place one spider orchid head into each glass jar and replace the lid.
6. Garnish with turkish coffee, spider orchids and sultanas.

CAUTION: Paper white flowers are not to be consumed.

(Substitute other flowers if flower ingredients are not available)

P.S. Makes a great Halloween gift.

a. cover the table with a table protection sheet and place 3 baby food jars with the lids off

b. place 1/3 of the packet of sultanas into each jar, keeping a few sultanas for garnishing

c, d. snap off the spider orchid heads and place one in each jar

f.

g.

e, f, g. Replace the lids on the jars. Garnish with turkish coffee, spider orchids and sultanas.

Cabbage Patch Flower

Cabbage Patch Flower Rated PG

Flower Ingredients

• Cabbage –Purple

• Kale –White, Green and Purple x 4

Flower Equipment

• Watermelon – Quarter

• Secateurs

• Plate

Method

1. Soak 2 leaves of purple cabbage in a bowl of hot water for 15 minutes.
2. Stand and allow to cool for 5-10 minutes.
3. Pat dry the cabbage leaves using a tea towel.
4. Using your secateurs, cut the bottom stem of the cabbage for flexibility.
5. Cut 20cm of string for container security.
6. With two hands, wrap 2 cabbage leaves around the plastic container, and with the help of a second party, wrap the string around the container. Tie a knot and bow for presentation.
7. Pour water half-way into the cabbage leafed container.
8. Cut to size kale, leaving 20cm of stem.
9. Place 4 stems of kale into cabbage container.
10. Garnish with petals of kale or cabbage coleslaw (optional).

(Substitute other flowers if flower ingredients are not available)

P.S. Makes a great Thank You gift.

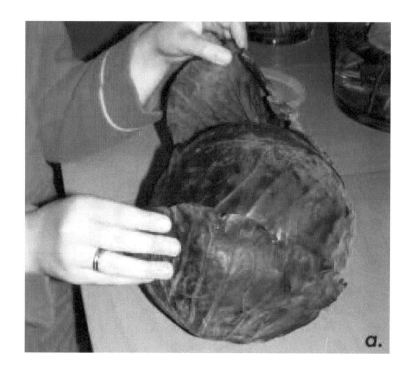

a. peel 2 leaves off the cabbage

b, c. place the leaves in a bowl and cover with hot water (ask for an adult to help). Soak the leaves for 15 minutes then allow them to cool for 5-10 minutes

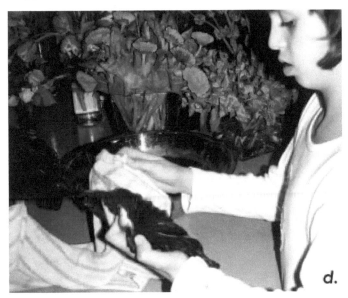

d. pat the cabbage leaves dry using a tea towel

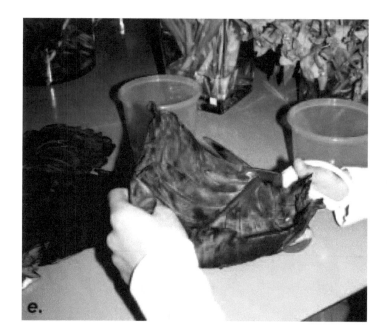

e. cut the stem of the cabbage leaves for extra flexibility

f. wrap the cabbage leaves around the plastic container

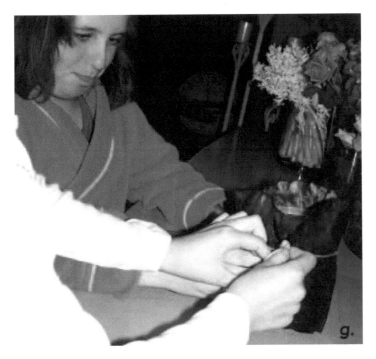

g. wrap string around the container and tie a knot and bow for presentation

h. pour cold water into the container up to half-way

i. cut the kale to size and place into the container

j, k. when you have placed 4 stems of kale inside the container adjust the positions until you are happy with how it looks

l. garnish with petals of kale around the container

Flowers
Down Under

Flowers Down Under Rated PG

Flower Ingredients

- Vanda Orchid – Purple

- Mini Roses –Orange/Yellow

Flower Equipment

- Watermelon – Quarter

- Secateurs

- Plate

Method

1. Place an empty spaghetti sauce jar on the table.
2. Using your scissors or secateurs, cut 10 small squares of cellophane.
3. Make a fist holding the cellophane. Feed the scrunched cellophane through the mouth of the jar, until the cellophane drops to the base of the jar.
4. Using your secateurs, cut off the vanda orchid heads.
5. Again, using your secateurs, cut the mini rose heads off their stem. Use as many flowers as you like.
6. Place some vanda orchid heads into the jar. Scrunch some more cellophane and feed it into the jar followed by the heads of the mini roses. Repeat the process until the jar is full.
7. Pour cold water up to the rim of the jar and replace the lids.
8. Cut about 20cm of purple ribbon and tie a knot and bow at the neck of the jar.
9. Garnish with leftover vanda orchid heads. *(Substitute other flowers if flower ingredients are not available)*

P.S. Makes a great Graduation gift for a loved one.

a. using your scissors or secateurs cut 20 small squares of cellophane

b. scrunch a piece of cellophane and place it into the jar

c. cut off the vanda orchid heads and the mini roses off their stems

d. place a vanda orchid into the jar on top of the scrunched cellophane

e. scrunch some more cellophane and place into the jar

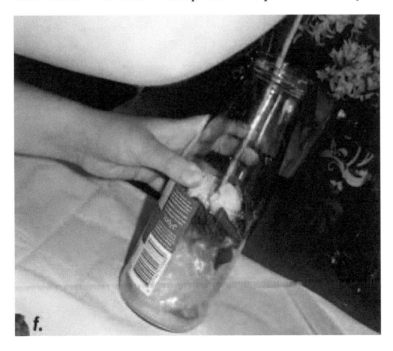

f. place some mini roses into the jar and use the stem of the rose to push the ingredients down into the jar

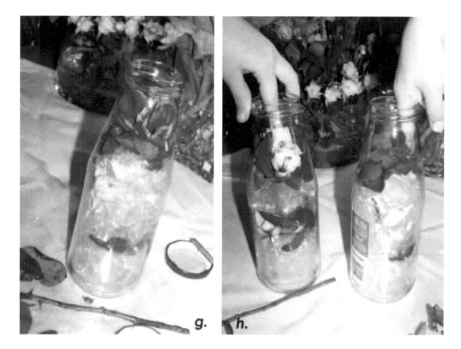

g, h. feed more vanda orchid, scrunched cellophane and mini roses into the jar until it is full

i, j. gently pour cold water into the jar until it is full

k. tightly screw the lid of the jar back on

l. cut about 20cmof purple ribbon

m, n. wrap ribbon around the neck of the jar then knot and bow.

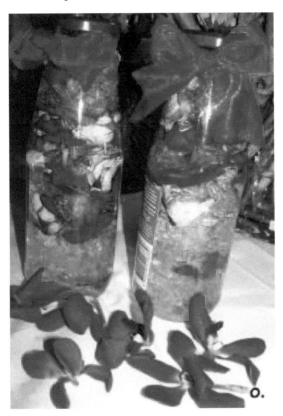

o. Garnish with left over vanda orchid heads

p. pose with your arrangement for a photo... lights, camera, flowers, enjoy!

Banana Flower Split

Banana Flower Split

Flower Ingredients

• Mini Sunflowers • Banana Leaves

• Banana Skins (optional)

Flower Equipment

• Foam Cup	• Stapler
• Floral Foam Brick	
• Butter Knife	• Secateurs
• Scissors	• Container
• String	• Table Protection Sheet

Method

1. Cover your table with a protection sheet. Using your secateurs, cut the banana leaf to size, enough to wrap around the foam cup.
2. Wrap the banana leaf around the foam cup and use the stapler to secure the banana leaf in place.
3. Cut a length of string and wrap it around the cup firmly, tie a knot and bow for extra security and dressing.
4. Measure and cut the Floral Foam bricks, to the size of the foam cup.
5. Place the cut floral foam bricks into a container of deep cold water, and allow to stand for 3 minutes.
6. While the Floral Foam brick is soaking, peel a few bananas. Keep the skin and eat the rest.
7. Shave off the edges of the pre-cut wet floral foam brick, so the floral foam can fit snugly into the foam cup.
8. Insert the wet floral foam into the foam cup and cover the mouth of the cup with leftover banana leaves.
9. Cut the mini sunflowers, leaving 10 to 15 cm of stem. Save the sunflower stems you have cut off.
10. Insert the sunflower stems into the banana leaf that covers the top of the foam cup and into the wet Oasis.
11. Garnish with banana skins and sunflower stems.

(Substitute other flowers if flower ingredients are not available)

P.S. Makes a great house-warming gift.

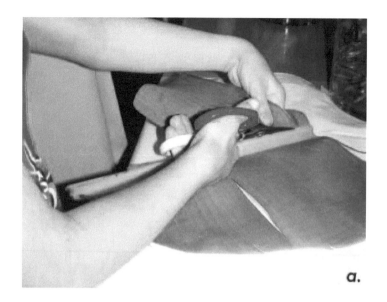

a. cut the banana leaf to size

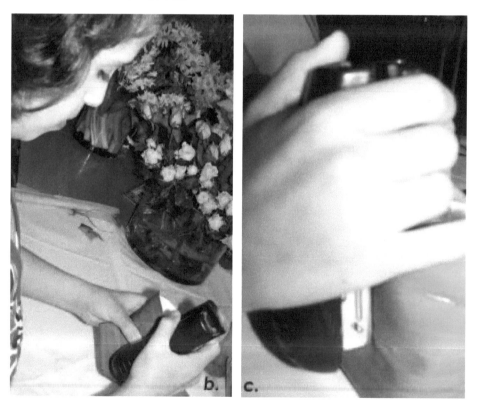

b, c. wrap the banana leaf around the foam cup and staple into position

d. cut off any excess banana leaf at the top of the cup

e. cut a length of string long enough to wrap around the cup

f. wrap string around the cup and tie a knot and bow to secure

g. measure and cut dry floral foam brick

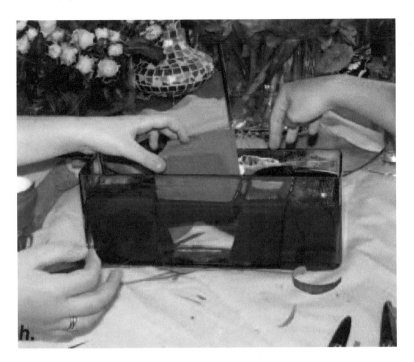

h. soak floral foam bricks in water for 3 minutes

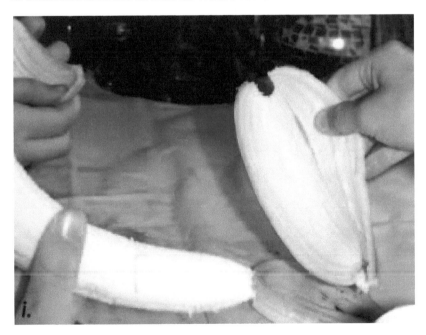

i. while the floral foam brick is soaking, peel the bananas and save the skins

j, k. cut the foam to fit and insert into the cup

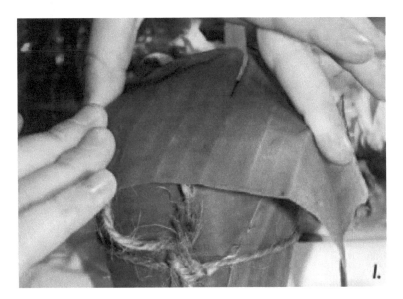

l. cover the top of the cup with a banana leaf

m. cut the sunflower leaving 10-15cm of stem

n. insert the sunflower stem through the banana leaf and into the wet Floral Foam Brick

o. Repeat with the remaining sunflowers

p. garnish with banana skins and sunflower stems

Flowering Pear

Flowering Pear Rated PG

Flower Ingredients

- Cymbidium Orchids

- Pears –Green

Flower Equipment

- 22 gauge Wire

- Mini Chisel• Secateurs

- Wire Cutters (optional)

Method

1. Place a pear on the table.
2. Insert a chisel into the side of the pear and make a hole.
3. Take a piece of wire and bend the tip to create a hook.
4. Using your secateurs, cut off the cymbidium orchid heads.
5. Holding a cymbidium orchid in one hand and the hooked wire with the other hand, thread the hooked wire through the mouth of the cymbidium orchid and once through, wrap the wire around the stem of the cymbidium orchid twice.
6. Using your secateurs or wire cutters, cut the wire, leaving 10-15cm of length.
7. Insert the wired cymbidium orchid into the side of the pear.
8. Using your fingers, feel whether the wire needs a further push for extra security.
9. Garnish with remaining cymbidium orchid heads.

(Substitute other flowers if flower ingredients are not available)

P.S. Makes a great Graduation gift for a loved one.

a. insert a chisel into the side of the pear and make a hole

b. bend the tips of the wire to create hooks

c. chisel out the remaining pears

d. cut off the cymbidium orchid heads

e. thread the wire into the mouth of the orchid and wrap wire around the base twice

f, g. insert the orchid into the side of the pear

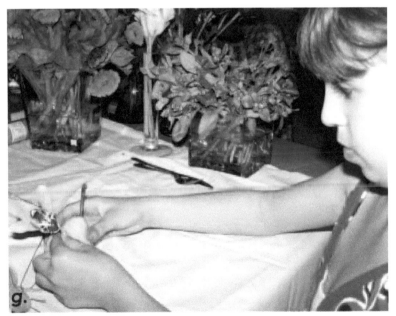

h. garnish with remaining cymbidium orchid heads

Mary Had A Little Flower

Mary Had A Little Flower

Flower Ingredients

• Lavender

• Cinnamon Bark

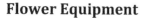

Flower Equipment

• Scissors

• Secateurs

• String

Method

1. Gather the bunch of lavender in your hand and, using your secateurs, trim the lavender to size.
2. Place 2 stems of Lavender in the inner side of the cinnamon bark.
3. Place a piece of cinnamon bark on top of the first one containing the lavender and make sure the lavender is secured in place.
4. Using your scissors cut 15cm of string.
5. Wrap the string around the cinnamon bark.
6. Tie a knot and bow for presentation.

(Substitute other flowers if flower ingredients are not available)

P.S. Makes a great Bon Voyage gift.

a. trim the stems of the lavender

b, c. place 2 stems of lavender into the cinnamon bark

d. cut a 15cm length of string

e. place a second piece of cinnamon bark over the top of the one containing the lavender

f. wrap the string around the cinnamon bark to secure

g, h. tie a knot and bow for presentation

The Milky Flower Way

The Milky Flower Way

Flower Ingredients

• Dendrobium Orchids –Lime Green and Pinkish White

Flower Equipment

• Plastic Baby Bottles x 3

• Baby Powder

• Pacifier

• Secateurs (optional)

• Sponge Paint Brushes

Method

1. Pour baby powder into two of the three bottles up to the 200ml mark on the bottles.
2. Pour baby powder into the third bottle up to the 150ml mark on the bottle.
3. Soak your sponge brush into water and squeeze out excess.
4. Insert your damp sponge brush into the bottle, wiping off the excess powder from inside and around the top of the bottle.
5. Using your fingers, pluck off the stem of the dendrobium orchids.
6. Insert the dendrobium orchids one after the other into the bottles.
7. Cap two bottles with their allocated lid and teat.
8. Cap the third bottle with a pacifier.
9. Garnish with leftover dendrobium orchids and baby powder.

(Substitute other flowers if flower ingredients are not available)

P.S. Makes a great gift for a Baby Shower.

a, b. pour baby powder into two baby bottles up to the 200ml mark

c. pour baby powder into the third baby bottle up to the 150ml mark

d, e. soak your sponge brush in water, squeeze out excess, then wipe off powder from inside and around the top of the bottle

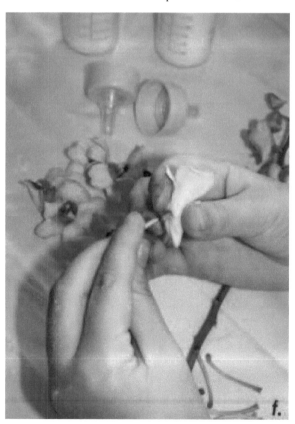

f. pluck the dendrobium orchid heads off the stem

g. continue plucking both the lime green and pinkish white orchid heads until you have enough for 3 baby bottles

h, i. insert a few of each colour of the dendrobium orchids into the baby bottles

j. once you have enough orchid heads in each bottle, cap two bottles with their lids

k. cap the third bottle with the blue pacifier

l. garnish with leftover dendrobium orchids and baby powder

Floral Quotations

- Let's plant a seed and watch it grow into a beautiful future of cut flowers.
- What's your floral signature?
- It is said, if you wake up to flowers, you are guaranteed a better start to the day.
- Cut flowers are like women –if you treat them well, they're more likely to stick around.
- They say you are what you eat and with cut flowers, they are what they drink.
- Remember to "slip on the heels and shave their legs" before placing your cut flowers into a vase
  Slip on the heels= cutting your stems on an angle.
  Shave their legs= removing any foliage below the water line.
- As race and colour represent people, cut flowers do too. A colourful and fragrant nation, waiting to embrace the world.
- Colour is like dressing on a salad, without it there is a difference. So let's add colour and have a feast.
- Make a start, make a difference and remember, good things come to those who flower.

Invitation to Share your work!

Everybody has their own style…we would love to see what you've created

Send through your designs to info@flowerarrangingforkids.com and we'll select 10 of the most creative each week and who knows we might create an amazing and magical online flower garden.

Don't forget that you can download your Free Flower Arranging Videos that go with this book at
www.FlowerArrangingForKids.com

CPSIA information can be obtained
at www.ICGtesting.com
Printed in the USA
LVHW080042030619
619931LV00016B/505/P